W9-AFK-570

American Symbols
AND THEIR Meanings

INDEPENDENCE
HALL

American Symbols AND THEIR Meanings

INDEPENDENCE
HALL

MASON CREST PUBLISHERS
PHILADELPHIA

Produced by OTTN Publishing, Stockton, N.J.

Mason Crest Publishers
370 Reed Road
Broomall PA 19008
www.masoncrest.com

3 5 7 9 8 6 4 2

Library of Congress Cataloging-in-Publication Data

Marcovitz, Hal.
  Independence Hall / Hal Marcovitz.
      p. cm. — (American symbols and their meanings)
Summary: Traces the history of Independence Hall in Philadelphia
and the documents brought there including the Declaration of
Independence and the United States Constitution.
  ISBN 1-59084-030-5
1. Independence Hall (Philadelphia, Pa.)—Juvenile literature.
2. Philadelphia (Pa.)—Buildings, structures, etc.—Juvenile
literature. 3. United States—Politics and government—1775-
1783—Juvenile literature. 4. United States—Politics and
government—1783-1865—Juvenile literature. [1. Independence
Hall (Philadelphia, Pa.) 2. Philadelphia (Pa.)—Buildings, structures, etc. 3. United States—History—Revolution, 1775-1783.]
I. Title. II. Series.
F158.8.I3 M37 2003
974.8'11—dc21
                                                    2002009578

Publisher's note: all quotations in this book come
from original sources, and contain the spelling and
grammatical inconsistencies of the original text.

American Symbols
AND THEIR Meanings

CONTENTS

Introduction

THE IMPORTANCE OF AMERICAN SYMBOLS

Symbols are not merely ornaments to admire—they also tell us stories. If you look at one of them closely, you may want to find out why it was made and what it truly means. If you ask people who live in the society in which the symbol exists, you will learn some things. But by studying the people who created that symbol and the reasons why they made it, you will understand the deepest meanings of that symbol.

The United States owes its identity to great events in history, and the most remarkable American Symbols are rooted in these events. The struggle for independence from Great Britain gave America the Declaration of Independence, the Liberty Bell, the American flag, and other images of freedom. The War of 1812 gave the young country a song dedicated to the flag, "The Star-Spangled Banner," which became our national anthem. Nature gave the country its national animal, the bald eagle. These symbols established the identity of the new nation, and set it apart from the nations of the Old World.

To be emotionally moving, a symbol must strike people with a sense of power and unity. But it often takes a long time for a new symbol to be accepted by all the people, especially if there are older symbols that have gradually lost popularity. For example, the image of Uncle Sam has replaced Brother Jonathan, an earlier representation of the national will, while the Statue of Liberty has replaced Columbia, a woman who represented liberty to Americans in the early 19th century. Since then, Uncle Sam and the Statue of Liberty have endured and have become cherished icons of America.

Of all the symbols, the Statue of Liberty has perhaps the most curious story, for unlike other symbols, Americans did not create her. She was created by the French, who then gave her to America. Hence, she represented not what Americans thought of their country but rather what the French thought of America. It was many years before Americans decided to accept this French goddess of Liberty as a symbol for the United States and its special role among the nations: to spread freedom and enlighten the world.

This series of books is valuable because it presents the story of each of America's great symbols in a freshly written way and will contribute to the students' knowledge and awareness of them. It is to be hoped that this information will awaken an abiding interest in American history, as well as in the meanings of American symbols.

—*Barry Moreno,*
librarian and historian
Ellis Island/Statue of Liberty National Monument

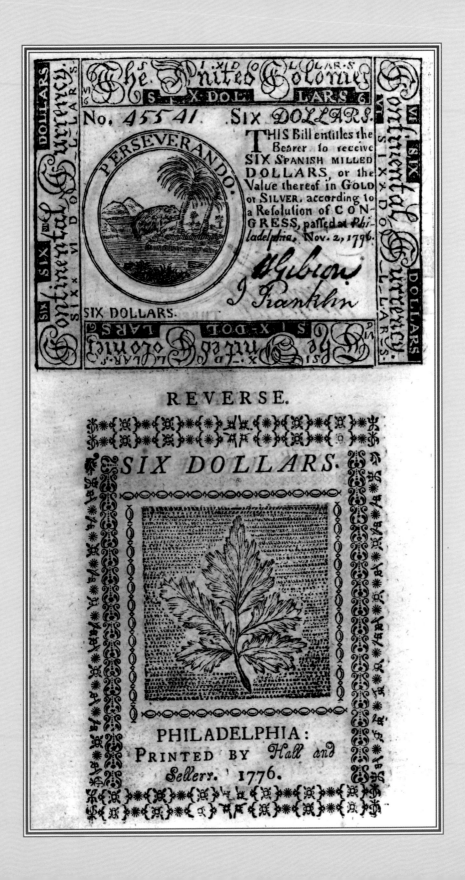

An example of colonial-era paper money, issued in Philadelphia in 1776. Nearly 50 years earlier, riots broke out in the city over the issue of paper money.

THE PAPER MONEY RIOT

*T*rading in paper money was rare in colonial America. Since there was little wealth in America, paper money often had little value. There were no great reserves of gold to give value to the paper money that was exchanged in place of precious metals.

However, as the colony of Pennsylvania grew, more paper money was needed in circulation. In busy Philadelphia, which had grown into the largest city in America, people needed paper money to buy food, clothes, tools, and other goods.

In 1726 King George appointed Patrick Gordon, an army officer, as *governor* of the colony of Pennsylvania.

The king cautioned Governor Gordon to be careful not to print too much paper money without true *assets* to give value to the *currency*. Doing so would mean that the money was worthless. So Gordon told the *Assembly* of Pennsylvania to draft a Paper Money Act—a law to increase the supply of paper money in the colony. But things moved slowly in colonial America, and the law would not be ready for three years.

Despite this, members of the assembly and many citizens called for the government to print more paper money. The issue was the subject of much debate on Philadelphia's cobblestone streets and in the city's *taverns*. Soon, Governor Gordon and the members of the assembly found themselves confronted by angry people demanding more paper money.

Sometimes, the demands turned violent. The paper money advocates recruited troublemakers from country

Patrick Gordon became governor of Pennsylvania in 1726. When he refused to issue new paper money to the citizens of the colony, some of them rioted. The Paper Money Riot, as it was called, nearly led to the removal of the colony's government from Philadelphia.

taverns outside Philadelphia to stir up trouble. Members of the assembly did not feel safe. They asked Governor Gordon to hold the next assembly meeting outside Philadelphia, in a safer place.

Before this time, there had been no actual meeting hall for the Pennsylvania's assembly. Philadelphia was the largest city in America, to be sure, but there were few public buildings. Occasionally, the assembly met in the city's courthouse or Quaker meeting houses. Sometimes, the assembly members were forced to decide the colony's business in private homes.

And so, while the assembly members searched for a safe place to meet outside the city, a group of law-abiding Philadelphians approached Andrew Hamilton and asked him to keep the government in Philadelphia. As assembly speaker, Hamilton led the legislature and was responsible for setting the *agenda* of the government. He decided which issues should be taken up by the members and oversaw various administrative duties.

The citizens of Philadelphia told Hamilton that if he moved the assembly meeting somewhere else, he would send a message that roughnecks were in charge. They submitted a *petition* to Hamilton, asking the assembly to set aside money to build a government meeting hall—a State House.

Meanwhile, the paper money *agitators* were not through causing trouble. Some members of the assembly who favored the Paper Money Act asked Governor

Gordon to approve £50,000 in new currency. (A pound, shown by the symbol £, was the unit of paper money used in the colony. This is still the name of a unit of money circulated in the United Kingdom.)

Months passed and Gordon still refused to issue new paper currency. On March 25, 1729, the assembly finally acted, authorizing £50,000 in new currency. But Governor Gordon issued a *veto* of the Paper Money Act—meaning he sent official notice to the assembly that he would not sign it. The governor's signature on the act was required for it to become law.

Assembly Speaker Andrew Hamilton helped put down the Paper Money Riot, designed the State House, and contributed in other ways to the growth of the colony of Pennsylvania. But his greatest accomplishment was the defense of John Peter Zenger, a newspaper publisher in New York who in 1734 dared to criticize Governor William Cosby.

There was no guarantee of a free press in 1734. Cosby was appointed by the king of England. He had Zenger arrested and tried for sedition, accusing the publisher of using his newspaper to stir up a revolution against the king.

Hamilton served as Zenger's attorney. "I cannot think it proper to deny the Publication of a Complaint which I think is the right of every free born Subject to make," Hamilton told the court. The jury was so moved by Hamilton's eloquent speech that it found Zenger not guilty. This landmark case is the basis for America's tradition of freedom of the press.

The agitators and troublemakers took to the streets of Philadelphia. Mobs tramped their way through the city, attacking citizens and breaking windows, doors, and street lamps. This night of violence became known as the Paper Money *Riot*.

The violence didn't last long. The ringleaders were soon arrested, and on March 31 Governor Gordon issued the Riot Act. This was a law that gave the governor permission to arrest and put to death people accused of starting riots. That helped quiet things down in the streets of Philadelphia and convinced the rioters to go back to their country villages.

With the paper money agitators back home in the countryside, the assembly finally took up the issue of the Paper Money Act. On May 1, 1729, the Provincial Assembly adopted a law giving Governor Gordon authority to issue £30,000 in new currency. And from the new currency, the assembly *appropriated* £2,000 to build a State House in Philadelphia.

A new country would one day be born in the State House—47 years later, members of the Continental Congress selected the State House in Philadelphia as the place where they would draft and debate the Declaration of Independence.

As for the building, it would come to be known as Independence Hall.

This colored illustration from the 19th century shows busy streets in front of the Philadelphia State House. The building is located on Chestnut Street, between Fifth and Sixth Streets.

THE STATE HOUSE

ennsylvania became a colony in 1681, when King Charles II of England granted land in the New World to William Penn to repay a debt the king owed Penn's father.

William Penn was a member of a religious group called the Society of Friends. They were nicknamed Quakers, because they were said to "quake" at the voice of God. Quakers faced religious *intolerance* in England. Many were imprisoned, including Penn. When Penn suggested to Charles that the debt could be repaid with land in America, Penn had in mind the establishment of a Quaker colony where people could worship as they pleased without fear of imprisonment. In Latin, the name Pennsylvania means "Penn's Woods."

Penn and the Quakers arrived in the New World in 1682 and founded a settlement along the Delaware River. Penn named the settlement "Philadelphia," a Greek word meaning "brotherly love."

Penn spent the next few years governing the colony, making land grants to settlers, and overseeing the development of Philadelphia. He drafted the "Frame of Government," an early attempt to establish a democracy in Pennsylvania, which included a General Assembly. Under the Frame of Government, members of the assembly were elected by the people.

Over the years, Penn revised the Frame of Government and in 1699 drafted a new version, which he named the "Charter of Privileges." Penn's charter would remain in place as the general framework for the government of Pennsylvania for the next 77 years. It ensured that a popularly elected legislature would meet to write the laws for the colony. However, the governor—who was responsible for carrying out the laws—would still be chosen by the king.

Penn had returned to England, where he died in 1718, by the time Pennsylvania's legislators found themselves immersed in the task of building a State House. The job of overseeing construction fell on a committee that included Assembly Speaker Andrew Hamilton, a physician named John Kearsley, and Thomas Lawrence, a political leader in the city who would go on to serve as mayor of Philadelphia. Hamilton picked the site, on Chestnut Street between Fifth and Sixth Streets, which at the time was on the western edge of the city. Between 1730 and 1732, the assembly acquired the land. Hamilton was a lawyer, but he also knew something about architecture, and he drew up the plans for the building.

Hamilton received help with the design from Edmund Woolley, a local carpenter who would build the State House and spend years maintaining the building for the assembly. The plan they developed called for a

The founder of Pennsylvania, William Penn was born in 1644 in London. While attending school, Penn became a Quaker. He was later arrested for his beliefs.

In 1681, Penn obtained a grant of land in the New World from the king of England in repayment of a debt owed his father. A year later, he arrived in North America and established a colony for Quakers which was called Pennsylvania. Penn envisioned the colony's main city, Philadelphia, as a "Greene Country Towne," and he assigned a surveyor named Thomas Holme the job of drawing plans for the settlement. Penn wanted the city's streets laid out in neat and orderly squares, unlike crowded, confusing London, where travelers had to negotiate narrow, tricky streets that often led in circles.

One of his greatest accomplishments was the writing of the "Charter of Privileges," which granted religious freedom to Pennsylvanians.

Penn eventually returned to England to aid Quakers still persecuted there. He died in England in 1718.

There was actually a "State House" in Philadelphia before the Provincial Assembly ordered a meeting hall constructed in 1729. In 1700, a home in the city occupied by William Penn was known as the "State House." After Penn moved out, it was used as a furniture store.

building that would rise two stories above the ground. The lower floor consisted of two large rooms: one on the east side of the building for use as a meeting hall for the assembly, and one on the west side intended as a courtroom for Pennsylvania's Supreme Court. The upper story included a long gallery. Hamilton saw this as a place where the public could gather for banquets and other events. Two other rooms would serve as offices for the governor and his assistants.

Woolley began work in 1732, enlisting the skills of local carpenters, joiners, brick masons, marble cutters, plasterers, and glasscutters. In 1733, the assembly members decided the building was not going to be big enough, and the members voted to alter the plans by adding east and west wings.

Construction moved slowly in colonial America. Tradesmen in the early 1700s had none of the modern tools that are employed today. Workers cut stone by hand. Materials were transported by slow horse-drawn wagons.

By 1736, the building was far from finished, but the assembly members decided it was well enough along for them to move in and start conducting the business of the colony. On October 14, 1736, the assembly held its first meeting in the new State House. The minutes of the meeting reflect that as one of the first pieces of official business in the new State House, Benjamin Franklin was appointed clerk of the assembly, after being "called in and qualified accordingly." In later years, Franklin would prove to be a dynamic figure in colonial Philadelphia, helping establish many of the city's institutions, conducting scientific experiments, and acting as a diplomat and statesman for the Continental Congress.

Meanwhile, work on the building dragged on. There were long delays in finding men and materials. In fact, even though the assembly members started using the State House in 1736, their meeting room would not be completely finished until 1745. The Supreme Court of Pennsylvania would not start presiding over cases in its courtroom until 1743.

Hamilton did not include a steeple in the original design, but in 1750 the assembly members told Woolley to add a bell tower and a flight of stairs.

In colonial America, bells were a very important method of communication. There were no televisions, radios, or telephones to carry messages to the people. There were a few newspapers, but most of them were published once a week. When citizens heard the *peal* of a bell, they knew to gather in a public square to hear important announcements.

An order for the bell was placed with Whitechapel Foundry in England. However, when it arrived in 1752 the new bell cracked on its first ring. Isaac Norris, who had replaced Andrew Hamilton as speaker of the Pennsylvania Assembly, hired John Pass and John Stow, two Philadelphia metal workers, to melt down the bell and recast it. They finished the new bell in 1753, but Norris was not satisfied with the sound of the bell's chime, so he ordered it melted down and recast again. Pass and Stow completed their task in a matter of weeks, but Norris was still not satisfied and ordered a new bell

Isaac Norris, the speaker of the Pennsylvania Assembly who headed the effort to obtain a bell for the steeple of the State House, was the son of a wealthy merchant who arrived in Philadelphia in 1692. Isaac Norris was raised as a member of the Society of Friends, the religious group known as the Quakers.

Young Isaac was educated for a time in England. By the time he returned to join the family business he was fluent in Hebrew, Latin, and French.

When Norris's father died, Isaac took over the family business and prospered. He became active in the government of Pennsylvania, becoming a member of the assembly in 1736 and speaker in 1750. Norris believed strongly in civil rights and felt the American colonies should be free. In 1751 he instructed the bell's foundry to inscribe the bell with these words: "Proclaim Liberty thro' all the Land to all the Inhabitants Thereof."

Norris would not live long enough to see independence. He became ill in 1764 and resigned from the assembly. He died in 1766.

After the State House was finished, a bell steeple was built and a grand bell ordered from England. The bell cracked the first time it was rung, so an American foundry was asked to melt it down and recast the bell. This large State House bell would ring to mark important events in the city—including the signing of the Declaration of Independence in July 1776. It would eventually be nicknamed the Liberty Bell.

cast in England. While waiting for the new bell to arrive, the Pass and Stow bell was hung in the steeple of the State House. It ultimately remained there for decades, even after the new bell arrived from England.

On July 8, 1776, the bell tolled following the first reading of the Declaration of Independence. The bell eventually gained its nickname—the Liberty Bell—from this historic day.

IN CONGRESS, JULY 4, 1776.

The unanimous Declaration of the thirteen united States of America.

When in the Course of human events, it becomes necessary for one people to dissolve the political bands which have connected them with another, and to assume among the powers of the earth, the separate and equal station to which the Laws of Nature and of Nature's God entitle them, a decent respect to the opinions of mankind requires that they should declare the causes which impel them to the separation.

We hold these truths to be self-evident, that all men are created equal, that they are endowed by their Creator with certain unalienable Rights, that among these are Life, Liberty and the pursuit of Happiness.—That to secure these rights, Governments are instituted among Men, deriving their just powers from the consent of the governed,—That whenever any Form of Government becomes destructive of these ends, it is the Right of the People to alter or to abolish it, and to institute new Government, laying its foundation on such principles and organizing its powers in such form, as to them shall seem most likely to effect their Safety and Happiness.

[The body of the Declaration continues in engrossed script, followed by the signatures of the delegates, beginning with John Hancock.]

One of the most important documents in American history is the Declaration of Independence. The Declaration explained why the American colonies should be free from Great Britain's rule. It was written in Philadelphia in the summer of 1776, and signed by members of the Continental Congress in Independence Hall.

DECLARING INDEPENDENCE

The sun rose over Philadelphia on the morning of July 4, 1776. It would be a hot and humid day in the city, but few people living in Philadelphia paid much attention to the weather. For months, the 56 members of the Continental *Congress* representing the 13 colonies had been meeting in their city. Although their talks were conducted in secret, there was little doubt about what they were up to: the drafting of the Declaration of Independence.

The Continental Congress had no home of its own. Delegates had been sent to the Congress by the governments of their colonies. At first, the Congress met at

Carpenter's Hall in Philadelphia, but in late 1775 the Assembly of Pennsylvania offered the much grander State House to the delegates. And that is where delegates arrived on the morning of July 4 to begin what they knew was quite likely the last debate on the declaration.

The colonies had been at war with the British since April 19, 1775, when the minutemen of Massachusetts fought against British soldiers during the battles of Lexington and Concord. Since then, the colonists had won important victories at Fort Ticonderoga in New York and Bunker Hill in Massachusetts.

Lately, however, the war had not been going well. General George Washington, the commander in chief, had asked for more troops, supplies, and ammunition, but the Continental Congress had no authority to provide Washington with the men and materials the general needed to fight the war. The delegates could only ask their legislatures back home to help the cause.

Still, the delegates aimed to break all ties with their British rulers, to declare America a free and independent nation.

That morning, the delegates entered the building

While the Continental Congress was meeting in the summer of 1776, it received a note from George Washington. The message said, "I must entreat your attention to an application I made some time ago for flints. We are extremely deficient in the necessary article." Flints were needed so the Continental soldiers could fire their muskets.

British troops fire on colonial minutemen near Lexington, Massachusetts, in April 1775. The "shot heard round the world" marked the start of the American Revolution.

through the large doorway facing Chestnut Street. Above the door hung the royal coat of arms—the final reminder to them that they were still living under the oppressive will of the king of England.

The delegates walked silently to the white-paneled meeting room on the east side of the building. Above, an elaborate crystal chandelier provided candlelight. There were two fireplaces in the room and tall windows lining the walls. Displayed in the room were a British drum, sword, and flag captured in 1775 by Continental Army soldiers under the command of Ethan Allen at the battle of Fort Ticonderoga.

At the front of the room was the president's *dais*—a

John Hancock was a wealthy merchant from Boston. He was one of the first patriots to support the movement for freedom from Great Britain. In 1776, Hancock was elected president of the Continental Congress, the body of colonial leaders who would write the Declaration of Independence.

raised table and chair usually occupied by the speaker of the Pennsylvania Assembly. On July 4, 1776, delegate John Hancock of Massachusetts sat at that table, having been named president of the Congress by the other delegates. Other delegates soon arrived, including Thomas Jefferson of Virginia, who wrote the Declaration of Independence while staying in a rented room in nearby Graff House; Benjamin Franklin, the printer, inventor, and statesman who had participated in many debates in this room as a member of the Pennsylvania Assembly; and John Adams of Massachusetts, who would go on to become the second president of the United States.

Just after nine o'clock in the morning, Hancock dropped the *gavel* to open the debate. One by one, delegates from the 13 colonies took their turns making their final arguments on independence.

In the final few days leading up to July 4, there had

not been unanimous support for the declaration. Delegate John Dickinson of Pennsylvania had urged caution. "When our enemies are pressing us so vigorously, when we are in so wretched a state of preparation,

Benjamin Franklin was a statesman, diplomat, inventor, and publisher. He started the first library in Philadelphia, and established the city's first fire company. He was no stranger to Independence Hall; his name appears in the minutes of the first meeting of the Pennsylvania Provincial Assembly held in the State House on October 14, 1736, when he was appointed clerk of the assembly. Later, he became a member of the assembly himself, winning an election in 1750. From that point on, he was a major influence on the politics and government of Pennsylvania, and later America.

In 1776, he helped to write the Declaration of Independence. During the debate on the declaration, Franklin made his famous warning to fellow delegates about the importance of unity. He said, "We must all hang together, or assuredly we will hang separately."

After the declaration was adopted and signed, Franklin served as a diplomat in France. He returned to Philadelphia in 1785. Two years later Franklin once again found himself participating in long debates in the State House. This time, his mission was to help draft the United States Constitution.

He died in 1790 at the age of 84. One of his last pursuits was establishment of the Philadelphia Abolition Society, which urged the government to outlaw slavery.

when the sentiments and designs of our expected friends are so unknown to us, I am alarmed at this declaration being so vehemently presented," he said.

Still, many delegates argued for independence. Delegate Caesar Rodney of Delaware rose from his seat and said, "As I believe the voice of my constituents and of all sensible and honest men is in favour of Independence and my own judgment concurs with them, I vote for Independence."

The debate continued. The declaration was read, changed and read again. Finally, a roll-call vote was taken. The vote was unanimous. One by one, the delegates stood at their desks in the State House and voted in favor of independence.

John Adams would later write: "I am well aware of the toil and bloodshed and treasure that it will cost us to maintain this Declaration, and support and defend these States. Yet through all the gloom I can see the rays of ravishing light and glory. I can see that the end is more than worth all the means; and that posterity will triumph in that day's transactions, even although we should rue it, which I trust in God we shall not."

At first, the declaration received just two signatures—those of Hancock, as president of the Congress, and Charles Thomson, the

> **Delegates debating the Declaration of Independence were pestered by horse flies that found their way into the State House from a stable across the street.**

In the Philadelphia State House, members of the Committee of Five—John Adams, Robert Livingston, Roger Sherman, Thomas Jefferson, and Benjamin Franklin—present the Declaration of Independence to John Hancock, president of the Continental Congress.

secretary. Later, the signatures of the other delegates were added.

Following its adoption, the declaration was sent to a printer to produce copies. Copies were distributed to a number of people the next day and sent to General Washington in the field. But for the most part, Americans were still unaware that their government had announced its independence from England.

On July 6, the Continental Congress met again and decided to announce on July 8 that the declaration had been signed. At some point on that day, probably at about 11 o'clock in the morning, the great bell in the State House steeple started pealing, calling citizens of

John Nixon reads the Declaration of Independence from a platform outside the State House on July 8, 1776. The Declaration had been signed on July 4—the date we celebrate as Independence Day.

Philadelphia to the public square for what was sure to be an important announcement.

Hundreds of citizens flocked to the public square. Just past noon on July 8, 1776, Colonel John Nixon, an officer in the Continental Army, strode out of the State House, climbed the steps of a rickety platform in the courtyard, and read the Declaration of Independence to the American people.

"We hold these truths to be self-evident, that all men are created equal, that they are endowed by their Creator with certain unalienable Rights, that among these are Life, Liberty and the pursuit of Happiness," Nixon read to the people gathered in the courtyard.

When Nixon finished reading the declaration, the bell in the State House steeple started ringing. In the crowd, people shouted: "God bless the free states of North America!"

And then nine soldiers from Pennsylvania marched to the Chestnut Street entrance of the State House. As hundreds of Americans cheered, the soldiers removed the royal coat of arms from above the door.

Later that night, the coat of arms was burned in a huge bonfire lit by the new citizens of America to celebrate their freedom.

Wrote John Adams: "The Declaration was published and proclaimed from that awful stage in the State House yard. . . . The battalions paraded on the Common. The bells rang all day and almost all night."

Every year, more than 3 million people visit Independence Hall and the Liberty Bell in downtown Philadelphia. However, during the early part of the 19th century, the building was used for purposes other than making laws. At one point it was almost demolished.

A New Purpose

ollowing the American Revolution, the State House in Philadelphia remained an important center for democracy. In 1787, the U.S. Constitution was written and adopted in the State House, providing Americans with a set of laws and a Bill of Rights.

Meanwhile, work started on a new federal *capital* on the Potomac River in Maryland and Virginia. The city, to be named the District of Columbia, would include the *Capitol*—a building where lawmakers would meet to carry out the young nation's business. The government was moved to the District of Columbia in 1800. It no longer needed the State House in Philadelphia.

The Pennsylvania Assembly didn't need it, either. In 1799, the assembly moved the capital of Pennsylvania to Lancaster, and in 1812 the capital was moved again to Harrisburg.

By 1816 the State House had fallen into neglect and desperately needed repairs. It was slated for demolition. But the citizens of Philadelphia stepped in and raised $70,000 to help the city government buy the building from the state government.

In 1824, the Marquis de Lafayette visited the State House. Lafayette was the French military general who helped lead American soldiers in the Revolutionary War. The marquis was still an enormously popular figure in America, where he was regarded as one of the true heroes of the war. Hundreds of Philadelphians turned out to greet the marquis in the old State House.

In 1824, the Marquis de Lafayette visited the United States, where the hero of the Revolution was greeted by cheering crowds. In Philadelphia, Lafayette visited Independence Hall. When the French general died in 1832, the Liberty Bell tolled to announce his passing.

The architect who saved Independence Hall from years of neglect was John Haviland, who was largely responsible for shaping the look of Philadelphia in the early decades of the 19th century.

Born in Britain in 1792, Haviland made his way to Russia in 1811 hoping for an appointment to the Russian Imperial Corps of Engineers. While in Russia he met John Quincy Adams, a future American president, who urged him to move to the United States. Haviland took Adams' advice and arrived in Philadelphia in 1816.

Haviland designed many of Philadelphia's most familiar buildings, including the Atwater Kent Museum, Walnut Street Theater, Pennsylvania Institute for the Deaf, and a former city hall of Philadelphia.

He is best known for his prison designs. Haviland was the architect for Philadelphia's old Eastern State Penitentiary as well as the Tombs (the city prison of New York) and penitentiaries in Missouri, Rhode Island, and Arkansas.

Monsieur Levasseur, Lafayette's secretary, wrote: "Mechanics with their hardened hands and uprolled sleeves, advanced to Lafayette; the magistrate and the plain-clad farmer stood together; the clergyman and the players moved side by side, and the children marched boldly along before soldiers and sailors."

Lafayette's visit to the State House awakened an interest among the people of Philadelphia and their city government to do something about the old building. Soon, they enlisted noted architect John Haviland to renovate the building and return it to its colonial-era condition.

They also decided to give the State House a new name. It would now be called Independence Hall.

Soon after Haviland finished work on Independence Hall, a New York newspaper had this to say about Haviland and what he was able to accomplish: "The best architectural taste in the country is found in Philadelphia, as her public buildings make manifest."

❧❧❧❧

In 1729, the Provincial Assembly of Pennsylvania appropriated £2,000 for the construction of the State House. Translated into modern dollars, historians believe it probably cost about $16,250 to build Independence Hall. The wings added onto the building in 1739 and 1740 cost another $12,000.

Today, the federal government owns the building. Independence Hall is part of Independence National Historical Park, and is maintained by the National Park Service. In 2001, the federal government spent about $13 million to maintain and operate the 45-acre park in downtown Philadelphia that includes Independence Hall and the nearby Liberty Bell Pavilion.

Independence Hall started its life as a place where lawmakers conducted the business of a government, but over the years it was used for other purposes. In 1740, the Library Company of Philadelphia, which was established by Benjamin Franklin, housed its collection of books in the State House. And during the American Revolution, the State House was used as a hospital for

Charles Wilson Peale was a well-known painter in Philadelphia during and after the American Revolution. He painted many portraits of Revolutionary leaders—including the painting of the Marquis de Lafayette found on page 34 of this book. During the early 19th century, after Independence Hall was no longer used for government purposes, Peale opened a museum of natural history in the building.

soldiers wounded in battle. In 1802, Philadelphia artist Charles Wilson Peale received permission from the assembly to open a museum of natural history in the State House. For the next 27 years, the building served as home to hundreds of specimens of plants, insects, birds, and reptiles. In fact, some of the exhibits were set up in the east room on the first floor—the same room where the Declaration of Independence had been debated and adopted. Peale posted a sign on the front door of the State House that read: "Here the wonderful works of the Divinity may be contemplated with pleasure and advantage. Let no one enter with any other view."

Today, there are no animal or plant exhibits in Independence Hall. Instead, it has become one of America's primary destinations for visitors. In fact, more than 3 million people visit Independence Hall and Liberty Bell Pavilion each year.

Abraham Lincoln was on his way to Washington, D.C, to be inaugurated as the 16th president of the United States, when he stopped in Philadelphia in February 1861 and spoke at Independence Hall. Lincoln can be seen at the center of this photograph, facing the camera.

LIBERTY TO THE WORLD

*I*n 1861, the nation was on the brink of civil war. For years, anti-slavery advocates in the North had called on the state governments in the South to abolish slavery. The southern states refused, and insisted on the *doctrine* of "states' rights," meaning they wished to decide for themselves whether to keep slavery.

The situation seemed hopeless. Already, violence had erupted. In Harper's Ferry, Virginia, armed men led by *abolitionist* John Brown attempted to rob an armory of the United States Army; their plan went awry and Brown was hanged. In Kansas, bloody *skirmishing* broke out between the pro- and anti-slavery forces.

On February 8, 1861, the Southern states formed the Confederate States of America and named their own president, Jefferson Davis. Soon, rebels in South Carolina would fire on Fort Sumter, touching off the Civil War.

Sadly, the nation that had been forged in the east room of Independence Hall on those hot summer days in 1776 now seemed sure to collapse.

On February 22, 1861—the birthday of George Washington—Abraham Lincoln stopped in Philadelphia. Lincoln was on his way to his *inauguration* in the District of Columbia, which had now been renamed Washington, D. C. The president-elect wanted to see Independence Hall—the place where the United States of America had been born. He did not expect to give a speech during the visit, but when word spread through the streets of Philadelphia that Lincoln was making a visit to Independence Hall, hundreds of citizens gathered on Chestnut Street and asked him to speak.

Lincoln gave in to their demands. He spoke briefly, but his remarks indicated his resolve for the job ahead of him—to preserve the Union by living up to the principles Jefferson, Adams, Hancock, and the other delegates had expected of all Americans when they met in Independence Hall some 85 years before.

> The basement of Independence Hall once served as the city dog pound in Philadelphia.

"All the political sentiments I entertain have been drawn, so far as I have been able to draw them, from the sentiments which originated and were given to the world from this hall," Lincoln said. "I have never had a feeling politically that did not spring from the sentiments embodied in the Declaration of Independence. I have often pondered over the dangers which were incurred by the men who assembled here, and framed and adopted the Declaration of Independence. I have pondered over the toils that were endured by the officers and soldiers of

The body of Abraham Lincoln lay in state in Independence Hall after his assassination in 1865; it was one of the many stops his funeral train made before the president was laid to rest in Springfield, Illinois.

the army who achieved Independence. I have often inquired of myself what great principle of idea it was that kept this Confederacy so long together. It was not the mere matter of the separation of the Colonies from the motherland; but that sentiment in the Declaration of Independence which gave liberty, not alone to the people of this country, but, I hope, to the world, for all future time."

1728 On February 20, citizens of Philadelphia ask the Provincial Assembly of Pennsylvania to establish a permanent State House in their city.

1729 The Paper Money Riot erupts in Philadelphia on March 25, convincing assembly members that they need a safe and secure headquarters for their government. On May 1, the Provincial Assembly of Pennsylvania appropriates £2,000 for construction of a State House.

1732 Work begins on the State House.

1736 The Pennsylvania Assembly meets for the first time in the State House on October 14; Benjamin Franklin is appointed clerk of the assembly.

1751 A steeple and bell are added to the State House.

1776 The Declaration of Independence is adopted in the east room of the State House on July 4.

1787 The United States Constitution is written and adopted in the State House.

1802 With Congress now meeting in Washington, D. C., artist Charles Wilson Peale turns the vacant State House into a museum of natural history.

1816 The city government of Philadelphia buys the State House, saving it from demolition.

1824 Following a visit by the Marquis de Lafayette, the State House in Philadelphia is renamed Independence Hall and renovated by architect John Haviland.

1861 President Lincoln delivers a speech in Independence Hall on way to his inauguration in Washington on February 22.

1950 National Park Service takes over ownership of Independence Hall from the Philadelphia city government.

1976 Liberty Bell moved out of Independence Hall to its own pavilion on January 1.

2002 A new pavilion is constructed for the Liberty Bell.

abolitionist—prior to the Civil War, an American who called for an end of slavery.

agenda—a formal list of things to be done or discussed at a meeting.

agitator—a person who stirs up others in favor of a cause, often urging violent action.

appropriate—to set aside an amount of money for a particular use.

assembly—the governing body of a state, composed of representatives elected by the people. The assembly is sometimes called the legislature.

assets—property of value that can be exchanged for money.

capital—a city that serves as the official center of government for a state or nation.

Capitol—the building in Washington where Congress passes laws and conducts other business.

Congress—a formal meeting of delegates or representatives to discuss matters of interest or concern.

currency—paper money or coins.

dais—a raised platform at the end of a hall or large room.

doctrine—a group of ideas that form the basis of beliefs or policies.

gavel—a wooden hammer used by a judge or presiding officer of a meeting to call order.

governor—the chief executive of a state or colony, responsible for carrying out the laws adopted by the assembly.

inauguration—the formal act of placing an official position upon a person.

intolerance—refusal by authorities to recognize religious rights.

peal—the sound made by bells.

petition—a formal request, usually signed by several people, made to a government for a specific purpose.

riot—a noisy and often violent public disturbance, usually caused by a group of people angered for a particular reason.

skirmish—a brief fight.

tavern—a café, bar, or inn, usually, where alcohol is served.

veto—the right to cancel an act of the government, usually exercised by a governor or president.

FURTHER READING

Kmeic, Douglas. *Individual Rights and the American Constitution*. Cincinnati: Anderson Publishing, 1998.

Marcovitz, Hal. *The Liberty Bell*. Philadelphia: Mason Crest Publishers, 2003.

Riley, Edward M., *Starting America: The Story of Independence Hall*. Gettysburg, Pa.: Thomas Publications, 1996.

Steen, Sandra and Susan Steen. *Independence Hall*. Englewood Cliffs, N.J.: Silver Burdett Press, 1994.

Weigley, Russell F. *Philadelphia, a 300-Year History*. New York: W.W. Norton and Company, 1982.

INTERNET RESOURCES

Information about Independence Hall
http://www.ushistory.org/libertybell/index.html
http://members.aol.com/bobbyj164/id7496.htm
http://www.nps.gov/inde/visit.html

History of the Declaration of Independence
http://www.ourdocuments.gov/index.php?flash=old&
http://www.loc.gov/exhibits/declara/declara1.html
http://www.yale.edu/lawweb/avalon/declare.htm
http://www.ushistory.org/declaration/

PICTURE CREDITS

BARRY MORENO has been librarian and historian at the Ellis Island Immigration Museum and the Statue of Liberty National Monument since 1988. He is the author of *The Statue of Liberty Encyclopedia*, which was published by Simon and Schuster in October 2000. He is a native of Los Angeles, California. After graduation from California State University at Los Angeles, where he earned a degree in history, he joined the National Park Service as a seasonal park ranger at the Statue of Liberty; he eventually became the monument's librarian. In his spare time, Barry enjoys reading, writing, and studying foreign languages and grammar. His biography has been included in *Who's Who Among Hispanic Americans*, *The Directory of National Park Service Historians*, *Who's Who in America*, and *The Directory of American Scholars*.

HAL MARCOVITZ is a journalist for *The Morning Call*, a newspaper based in Allentown, Pennsylvania. He has written more than 20 books for young readers. He lives in Chalfont, Pennsylvania, with his wife, Gail, and their daughters, Ashley and Michelle.